SPRING

IN

NAME

ONLY

SPRING
IN NAME
ONLY SOME NEW AND OLDER POEMS

TODD
SWIFT

BLACK SPRING **POETRY**

First published in 2020
by The Black Spring Eyewear Press Group
Suite 333, 19-21 Crawford Street
Marylebone, London w1h 1pj
United Kingdom

Typeset with graphic design by Edwin Smet
Cover painting by Edwin Smet
Selfie by the author
Printed in England by TJ International Ltd, Padstow, Cornwall
in a limited first edition print run of 400 copies only.

The right of Todd Swift to be identified as author of
this work has been asserted in accordance with section 77
of the Copyright, Designs and Patents Act 1988

isbn 978-1-913606-29-9

**ALL SALES PROFITS GO
TO THE WORLD HEALTH
ORGANISATION**

i.m. POETS
AL ALVAREZ
CIARAN CARSON
ELAINE FEINSTEIN
LEAH FRITZ
RODDY LUMSDEN
WILLIAM OXLEY

with thanks to some dear friends:

Cate
Edwin
Fr. Oliver
Jordan
Martin
Patrick
Peter
Phil
Suetonius
Thor

And of course, always,
Sara!

B
P   S
E

Note, an earlier version of this collection was far longer,
and probably self-pitying. I have (for now) expunged those poems,
exposed by the Pandemic, to be at least momentarily trite, or too much
about Brexit, to refocus the collection on neo-modern and neo-romantic
poems, that better express the concerns of the present age. I have also
added new poems, and brought this version up to the end of May.
I have retained some light verse, and also poems of desire, love, and
doubt, that capture the relative frivolity of a time now seemingly
distant, but poignantly recent, if only for nostalgia's sake.

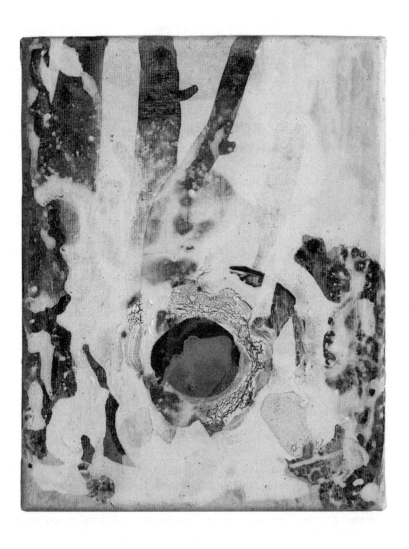

'I was going down,
was gonna drown
then I started swimming.'

– Adrian Borland, 'Winning'

TABLE OF CONTENTS

'I SEE THE HURRICANOES'

I see the hurricanoes
and then turn to the drop
of rain that bides its modesty
on a vanquished leaf, trembling
in fear at the expediency of water;
O duplicitous conquering creeper, I
declare – never have I encountered more
dapper conniving in a Machiavel bead of weather
before now – and in the comparison am dry indoors.

YOUTH IN JULY

It sounds sentimental, and I suppose it is,
Like Swinburne in Putney, Watts-Dunton
Babysitting the dipsomaniacal spanker,
Devotedly praising children in his dotage,

The verse no longer about outré vampires,
Yet here, in my July garden, Wimbledon
On the telly like a never-aging stone
Idol the islanders kowtow to, until

A messy anthropologist uncorks the wine,
Spoiling the bottle by spilling contents
Best-left unexamined – well, that's gone awry,
There's no religion in tennis love can't cure;

I meant, the sound of schoolkids, shocking
In its tsunamic waves, a busload or six
Unloading the (unseen) catcalls, shouts, cries
Of excited innocence (or thereabouts),

As they head to the nearby recreation ground,
To compete for ribbons in the temperate sun,
On the same track Bannister trained on,
All those innocent years ago, when climbing,

And running, other sports, added coronation
To the empire and its outlying parts – Larkin's
Innocence, which was shabby and mired after all
In grumpy muck and semi-ironic racist slurs –

Time blurs, from one compromised poet to the other;
Who can fault a talented mind for going blurry
During time's declining flurries?
Once, we knew humans to be human, hence,

Less than perfect, if even perfectible; current
Hubris is to aim for robot superiority and beyond,
A *Toy Story* with the moral batteries included;
And Britain is good at batteries, they will save

The planet in the not-too-distant...
More proximate, and today, the incredible
Loudness of what could be a thousand kids
Just beyond my mansion block's walls and fence,

Lifts and falls, like Arnold's tide, a man
Well-trained to appreciate athletic youth,
And what a civilisation requires to do well abroad;
My touchstones are imperfect memories

Of certain lines from verse composed by those
Who turned out to be wholly or in part perverse;
And none the worse for those readings, I remain,
Not sane and not unverbose, thrilled to the bone

To hear the unmediated joy or nuttiness
Of the much younger, running to a day of games;
A sound as old as Athens, it may be, if not
Quite as attic, antic, purely classic, or the same.

VERLAINE, LONDON AND PARIS

In the bedroom of violence
you can find reverence
like a broken crucifix;
get your fix with a sucking kiss;
boy of my pains, reveries since
blown away like vaping,
where have your blond bangs
gone? Have you found
a new brutality to be mastered
by? Do you lie down daily
to be profoundly violated
purely for fun, for pleasure?
Do you measure memories
as I do my pornographics?
Oh the moon and sun
vie for attention, neither wins;
so too do human sins circulate
on a spin cycle like a machine
to wash our amities away.
Poets who vacillate die anyway;
looking for trophies is idiotic;
you don't come to heaven
it comes to you in a loin's
lion-like roar; spasm of brain
and bodies; it bodes well
when we entwine like Romans
praying in a delicious orgy
at the infernal Vatican.
I am an unrepentant lover
of chapped lips and escape;

I enjoy youths with acne,
lounging about like louts.
Shouts and we arrive, in French,
on the English shore; passion
speaks in two languages,
bilingual like our mixing fluidity;
you're beauty air-flown
into my dropbox; you never left
my Left Bank alt-right thug;
I plug up the holes in my leaking
heart with bark and gum;
your opposable thumb up
my appreciative bum. Bless
you my genuine maniac,
your menace crashed my laptop,
your writing killed me hot Brutus.
Just us lost in lust, Lotos lollers.
Because desire fulfilled is a cup
that is a generous publican.
At the end they make me a statue,
but your marbled thighs lay
more profoundly in eternal gratitude;
satiation is only a faun lapping
regularly at the joyous pool,
cooled by ferns and fed by Venus;
there is only one word here to rhyme;
and in time it lengthens, his, mine;
ah we mined the deep earth so well;
to grip diamonds first impress coal;
from stressure get treasure;
I lick thy milk bowl, the razored cat
with a bird in each pocket, allied
to the lugubrious rat. Go home

now boy, it has gotten late in paradise;
and I must operate heavy machinery
tonight, to make the stars move,
industrious billionaires ensnaring
all they befriend with nets alight!

GOVE IN LOVE – IRREGULAR SONNET

I give to you my three line whip
to compel me to do as you bid me to;
in this teamed way my heart runs true
to how any dog on fox would obey
or unleashed at least not misconstrue
how to foaming bare a fanged lip,
for a team whipped-in cannot stray
far from freedom's complex clip,
which has been portrayed as tennis
nets, that regulating presence in lieu
of force that enhances play;
thus, overmastered in your cabinet,
sir and madam may come to blows
with passionate support for Brexit
or any new perversity they propose.

3 CASTINETS

1

if there is a day
more melancholy
than the first one
in September
tell me
i want to meet it
and say
i know your twin
whose coming
is sadder
than winter
you standing
opposite to spring
the both of you
trouble-bringers
cry-making
you close summer
like a loved book
and return it
to a far-off library
overdue like snow.

2

the days of light
i thought of film actors
who had played killers

or boys or strange
men in the nineteen
fifties and sixties
often in european
or lower budget
productions, some
with Welles, like Dean
Stockwell and Anthony
Perkins; and of John
Dall who died after London
and that odd fall;
others like Clift – all
attractive to me doomed
in my august bed of sun
with a black cat blazoned
at my feet like a sigil.

3

The twilight of the pool toys
comes without napalm
or spritz – it's tame, the whimper
when air poofs out the swan
and a rather long banana
disimproves in size; a dwindled
best friend to Caesar on
if waving water in lungwise;
Ling Po or his brother's son
saw their moonface, drank
up their face. Narcissus
is a bad kisser. Pow.
It's sadder than Dad this now.

Like younger days of lustrousness.
Now the day slips their dress;
the night port takes a dimmer view
of this, that, them, her, him, me, you.

OCCASIONALS

I

On the bus from Pembroke
I see them kiss, passing,
kids from school, one in red;
Housman had said a pessimist
was what he was, not just
a classicist, well-read, serious;
and he was right when he spoke
thus, for time's harassing
has made of his body only dust;
a brutal feast after the quietus;
the grave is dismal, tedious,
and crass. No after-dinner talk;
love is a fast glance glimpsed;
then sped away. Amassing
fortune or must, famed or broke;
it's the same fate for living
and the late; merely the timing
changes, the inscribed dates
thrust upon the marble block.
I'm happy for the lovers
and wish them hours awake
among the roses of their bed.
The alternative is simply dread.

2

Treat everyone you meet
like your father lying
in a hospital bed
dying of brain cancer;
you are leaving the country
in an hour – now
is your only time
with him, with him.
Stay as long as you can.
The taxi is waiting but...
you have your differences.
It is now and never.
Love is all that is left
in this room of curtains.
Be gentle with yourselves.

3

The beauty of being
an unknown poet
is that the world
and time still
have all the time
in the world
to discover you
and how much of
a thrill that will be
for them
when they find
new love
in your old words.

4

Now that I am defeated
I can join
the long list
of all who came before
and also fought
the waves, the law,
to break on stone
or buzz saw;
the splinter in my paw
has grown man-sized;
I am only alone
in my mind. Created
by hate, all hate is poor.
It is hardcore this kiss
you hand me with your
private lies, public fist.
I will pray and fast,
weep and tear away.
What stays after all is gone
may, please, be better pain.

5

in heat
in full heat
in oven heat
in Miami heat
in wild palms heat
in house on fire heat

in mad movie mogul heat
in the day of the iguana heat
in mission control blast-off heat
in odd July London what next heat
in heat I feel more alive
than at any other time
except when jumping
deep into the cold cold lakes
of Northern Quebec I love

REDDEST OF REDS

imponderable red
red deep as rood
rudest red
brick red
rose dying of red
redder red
1970s red
silent red
the saddest red
blush red
kiss red
cinnamon red
mother red
invasion red
ruddy red
Jesus red
constant red
thermometer red
convoluted red
red before bed
red in the west
breast red
hottest red
cold cold red
shovel red
poem red
medical red
redder than Mars
red as the inner sun
well red

hat red
redder than cherries
beyond any red known
the farthest red
incorrigible red
red as a way of life red
the red forgotten
the red of a nation
national red
red velvet
red is missing
reductive red
red as the rose I saw
red as Sara
red as a knife
rudderless red
mayhem red
stinging red
red sea
red fish
red school
red submarine
red tan
redress red
ruined red
all the reds I refuse to name
nameless red
dread red
murder red
regret red
red as the fire
that redrew the map

LITTLE POEM

It is a matter of some concern
that I can't seem to learn,
despite my daily Wiki fix,
the difference twixt MI5 and MI6.

ENGLAND AFTER THE SNOW

The snow fell, closing all schools
across the land. It cloaked halls

and spires, law courts and mosques.
It hit radio masts, falling small but fast.

It coated statuary, brave and young
caught in brusque past battles

across the channel. The snow lasted.
Children and tutors colluded with balls

in the street, colliding like fools
in love with tumbling and attack.

There was no lack of snow around.
The floor became a cold cold ground.

The shadow cabinet rolled out a man
of three parts, round, with a mace

for a nose. The snow never stopped.
It had hardly begun. It propagated

like an evolution experiment of bacteria
dividing their minute cells. Like unwanted

men and women who had snuck in,
across borders, it rose, a sort of wall.

of sound and noise. Furious falling snow.
Faster, faster. Soon the nation was

entirely white out, cheering some
quarters more than others. For those

who felt more excluded by this revisionary scene
of pure deep cleanliness like wedding linen,

it was an affront to difference, to bright
tones rich with inflected colour, various shades.

There was a great need for change they said.
The fanatic with a webcam knows

what does not melt becomes black ice
or other bitter forms of concealed vice.

The play in the glittering frozen parks
roused a few to tint the carpet streaks of red.

The monumental blood rose of winter spread.
The serene crystal magnificence of sunlight

caught in a branch among strong icicles shone
across the prime minister's lawn, dividing it

like a pen marking an essay, between the paragraphs
that worked and those that failed to convey the meaning.

Half was scuffled footfall after a brawl between drunken
hangmen wanting their fall guy and the other was blank

as a paper cheque, quaint in its formal emptiness,
like the promise of a religion that never built a church

or held a ceremony, unable to locate any clergy.
If you stood out in the general wind and clutter

of the endless whiteness of the enduring snow
and were still like a mannequin or a scarecrow

then you became cold and alone like marble from Italy,
worked into an exquisite figure of carved artistry,

out of a fabled moment when the hand and eye
and purpose could unify for beauty and intent,

without the design failing any concern,
or leaving the visited heart discontented.

POEM IN THE STYLE OF

They say that death is final
And I am unsure
Since records traced on vinyl
Once dusted now endure

In newfound circles
Where the old is saved
As refreshed miracle,
A child out of the grave.

It cannot be so simple
Whether soul end or start
At birth's gothic steeple,
When we know, a bit, the heart

Is without an easy entry point;
It flows in roundness, like
Water has no centre to anoint;
You hold a flood with a dyke.

It breaks and then all life is in
At once, so death;
One's grave is just an even sin;
It lies about our deeper breath.

Mother's day, 2018; Cambridge and London.

REMEMBER NOTHING IS MORE BOISTEROUS

than a poem
alehouse to the stars
an eruption of indexent proposals

and vague rumours
hustled across a vast apparatus
in a rush

the largest happenings
spread like a flowering basket
at the end of August;

it is difficult
to articulate exactly
why being precise is vital

to improve the civilisation
we somehow pass on;
religion and the sky

gesture at eternal
thought experiments;
the wry lothario

or sodden wino
know a different transubstantion;
god is the grape and the press

that exudes the wine;
make of it what you will
summer is intoxicating,

is divine. It returns
and takes us like all gods.
Is cruel and generous

as it wishes. Is sudden
and long then goes.
The wind is a god

and the rain. But not
the summer god
who reverberates as thunder

does and shakes us
from sleep to threaten
wind and rain and more.

What encompasses everything
is more. And so you have definition
of our Lord. And our own

limits of adoration and demise.
We own the earth from hell
to heaven. And nothing else.

The summer shimmer-shudders,
a louche swan riding the girls of vehemence
who are the artful heirs

of the districts where trees move;
bear with me. I am drunk, will go
soon. I mean only to charm you

for some alms. Some small comfort
in this pandemic of a world.
Is not the sun good and calm?

4 SONNETS FOR ERIC, WHO LIVES IN A LONDON HOSTEL

I

In terminable pain I see God's eye.
He favours me, in silent radiology.
I cry for peace, he fastens on a sword.
His breathe is but a limpet-word.
Angels haul gross demons to the feast.
In love I see this love is my least
possession, to give on to a heating kiln.
Being born is meant to raise our cry.
Crowds glimmer all around me,
I walk in division, a burning raiment
around shoulders like pure cold.
I am killed daily in slaughterhouses
of oxen, where halfway men
are kennelled by worldly lowering –

2

fed barely, like a forgotten kid;
I weep like a torn coverlid; sleeping
in the hostel on a razor's bed,
dreaming of how not to bleed;
fear is my companion of the sheets;
I doze between rows steep with men,
Lord, who cannot lift again
themselves back to even broken;
our bridges are all fallen down
in eminent indifferent London-town.

There is no money to take a wife;
and I am unskilled, except in memory;
I'll recall each unkindness a full life;
my mind is set, a ringing seismograph;

3

it twitches at the mouse's laugh;
the cat's jibe, pavement's spitted curse;
we live beside a parlour, its hearse
rounds like clockwork, bearing
fortunate applicants to their benefits;
each soul given not what it needs;
only what Mammon can spare today;
it's thin gruel, a small slice of night;
you're on your own, and more alone
than even that signifies; removed
often even from your own mind;
left precisely nowhere solid, citizen,
lost on a corner to prattle for pound,

4

to get pence; coins otherwise destined
for a lotto ticket or the *Telegraph*;
release me from beggary, pleading, going
old or blind, or both, any thing;
I live miles to where someone is king;
none of that kingdom rolls as far
as I lie; prettified seasons sorted high;
there's castles, carriages, soldiery,

a glistening presence in the chancellery;
water in bottles costing more than bread;
it's madness sold like silken thread,
woven around the exchequer's heads;
spend me God, in the sun, make of me
a seed of rain. I wish to spin, risen,
to pivot up as golden growing grain.

MOVE INTO THE LONG LIGHT CAUTIOUSLY

move across the day with alacrity,
take care as you go among hours;
each second bears a grief to come,

time carries a toxin potent as curare;
no cure for the summer solstice;
your poultice is useless given night

will swing into action, after minutes
give way to the eventual moon;
midnight is noon's anti-pope;

the rope of our calendar hangs us
out to dry; even Jesus was born
before, or after, his own anno domini;

each baby has a cry; I recall
the stories I was handed, about
being strong, brave, and too small;

barely surviving becomes a mark,
a driving force; how to unwind
when we're all wound to spring

back, like a recalcitrant clock?
I've had the hard knocks, you bet;
been dangled in Vulcan's net;

torture, check; humiliation, roger that.
You don't need to be a soldier
to suffer captivity, wounds, fear.

The sunlight as it patrols the dial
does all the damage we require;
the sun's trial never pardons;

we fall into the prison's clutches;
the dark side of any solstice
is its end, the next outcrop

of just more of the same, the long
slow rolling out of the panthers, tigers,
lions, and the rest of the roaring circus.

It's a circuit, and each ring's rampant
with wildlife on display; some talons
cross paws, leap for the peanut gallery;

in the festooning blood it's natural
to try to flee; you needn't bother, son,
daughter, the hourglass loses sand

but only to tip upside down, slog on;
we're all in the tropics as one big cargo;
the rays beat beat beat down down down.

YOU COMING HOME

to the closing day's light
like it was the 1950s
or some new model world,
in your Aquascutum
to lift our five pounds of sugar
cat in the garden;
a stillness only money buys;
and we know the cost
also of noise;
near-broken, we mend
like Muldoon's trees,
arms around each other,
the human tether
in this twilit time
of coming terror.

June 17, 2019

LIFE IS INCREDIBLY SAD. I REFLECT ON THIS

as a point of comfort when being bullied
in the arena of our age. I dwell especially
on the face of my father, lying in his coffin.
My first impression was not that he was sleeping,
but how beautiful he was, and temporary.
I had thought him an eternal thing.
My first major death was my father's.

In life, he was, as they say, complex. The troubled
analyst Masud once wrote that the human is a paradox,
not to be cured but understood.
Looking over my father, I understood only
that he was now beyond reproach, and further pain.
And that he had been finite, after all.
Life is the paradox of immeasurable eternity, and then
blunt terminal velocity. Living is a constant fall;

we hope we are falling from a greater not a lesser height.
Some die in infancy. Playing in my garden today with my cat,
I recalled my Aunt Bev, who has been dead for more years
than this century. She was once at the heart of my life;
my kindest ally; a sensitive and bookish presence;
with great affection for animals; and a shyness that meant
she probably got less from her life
than she may have hoped. I believe she had a gift for reading

and discussing and would probably
have been a good poet; but crippling insecurity kept her
from writing much, though she once won
a school prize for a story. When I write poetry it is for her.
I think of her now, as I am in the mild sun

of late May here in London, and I think that,
despite the bullying, bad news, cruelty,
and general nasty edge of this time,

the sadness is truer and more beautiful –
the sadness is, I once knew such people,
such lovely people. Their chill shades
blow through me now, and move me,
and I am no longer afraid of phantoms,
for I have seen what the brute reality really does;
no bully can take my father now, or my loved ones,
already gone, who were so gentle, and deserved so much love.

IN MEMORIAM, I.M. PEI

See clean buildings
In the mind
Made perfection
To shape sun
Light
Or its opposition
The eye inside
Makes ideal
The lying shade
Outlines
An infactual shielding
Genius can provide
Outside it stays
Granite steel glass
Paid for
A construction
From a chosen plan
Like a tree
Or mountain
Natural if taken
From imagination
To be said in space
Art is what limit
Is chosen
To be broken
And remade
It need not be great
Measures
A new stride
Geometry is its own kind

Of portion
What happens in the end
Is displacement
The air moved
Aside
To somewhere else
The presence
Of an architected
Thing is like
An ended storm
The proportionate palace
Thinking

A construction
A new stride
An ended storm
An infactual shielding
And remade
Art is what limit
Aside
From a chosen plan
From imagination
Genius can provide
Geometry is its own kind
Granite steel glass
In the mind
Is chosen
Is displacement
It need not be great
Light
Like a tree
Made perfection
Makes ideal

Measures
Natural if taken
Of an architected
Of portion
Or its opposition
Or mountain
Outlines
Outside it stays
Paid for
See clean buildings
The air moved
The eye inside
The lying shade
The presence
The proportionate palace
Thing is like
Thinking
To be broken
To be said in space
To shape sun
To somewhere else
What happens in the end

NEW POEM AS MY BIRTHDAY APPROACHES

If my cat needed advice, but Suetonius needs none,
I'd start with Alvarez, who told me Sylvia's summa:
The Small Say No, The Big Say Yes.
Last year suggests it's best to tamp down tempers,
Never fire the social media flare gun, or go on
Any computer, much. To reflect before going gaga
Over abandoning one union or another; consider
The narrow margins and swing seats as opinion
Swells, divides like a collapsing wave post-Exodus;
It's not like us, feline or human, to be always kind,
Or know our several minds. We leap, skitter, replace
One severed mouse or bird with yet another, chase
A costly raising of the gambit. But it's not poker,
Or the ice in the bourbon Plath called *that sound
Of America.* A nice flourish, her recollection; yet,
In twenty years, who will recall Dean or Monroe,
Presley or Manson, Arnolds Palmer, Schwarzenegger?
The pace of the current online jolt, the digital rush,
Is crushing to what's encompassed by contemplation
Of prayers, poetry, solemn chimes; untender spring.
It's looking like a mess, then a mush, then a lurch
Over any cliff you've got on offer. We're Babeling
Via Babylon on the way to a conflagrating church;
The spire itself is on fire, the crow's nest below
Sea-level. I turn a bit older without an heir apparent,
To warn, or wish better things may come again; except,
I sense it would be wiser to prepare for pure neglect
Than dominion of our angels, with what I've heard
Of demons that we dream of, and how even kittens
That I adore, find sweetest, will ruin mostly any bird.

For ruination can enter into history's glade by love as well
As anger; dismaying, to be sure, but everyone is in danger
Now, like we move about in air; we're breathing in
The intoxicant of these damaging years; the obnoxion
Of fumes wafting like skunk out of neighbours' windows;
I'd advise a young cat to retract fine claws, but extend
Keener senses anyway, as everywhere fluent she goes
May carry chance of hawk or poacher's fastening pain,
Across the sun-capped moraines, capitulating floes.

April, 2019

THE MOUNTAIN

After A.M. Klein

The mountain held the holy college
Where we learned to think of ourselves
As higher than before, though we lay down
At night in the coming dew, to roll in glass

And talk to you, to talk sweetly to you,
In hopes that your pretty beauty, careless
As youth will be, would turn to reflect
How we wanted to appear in your view;

Around about were cemeteries, Jew
And Gentile understood to be gone;
An old hospital where I had been born,
Too small to leave in a mother's shawl;

We read long books and yearned to kiss,
Among white trees that offered logic
To the seasonal pining of young men;
Telling, as snow reversed resurrection

And returned to the ground, O Wedekind
In Montreal! – gash, gall! – helium!
Ties as thin as finger bones; Austro-
Hungarian lips, and girls asleep in coffins,

Joy Division brutal dance band of the age;
We broke red bottled wine, to make
The soil on this mountain a simple stage
On which to complicate our bodies,

TODD SWIFT

Each offering over to you this cross,
Stretching passion of our lovelorn fire,
The need to become mortal in desire's skin.
Susan, loved you fiercely as a Montreal frost.

ALLEN TATE

I am thinking of Allen Tate's large head.
His leaves twirled about the recent dead.

He loved the ladies overmuch it is said.
Is this why he is no longer very much read?

The Fugitives have lost much of their cred.
It may be because the agrarian soil has bled,

Or that time simply moves on, bed by bed
Where lovers and critics have all fled.

POEM FOR SUETONIUS KITTEN

The black grit
in the eye
is the news

a beam daily
to bear;
come the smallest

smudge of life
in the Bombay
kitten (uncontrollable

sentimentality
on the furry floor)
all gets funny;

the world still smut
and drudge, smash,
grab, and extreme

in all extremities –
call it the compass of shit.
But, here is a ball

of nutty profession
of what else is natural:
hilarity of purpose,

yet claws serious
as political shame;
he does what all do:

inhabits like a hostile takeover
that is smiles, too.
Happiness scribbles white;

at night he writes sleepless
pummel horses on my skull.
No one else is allowed

to bite my good books;
he has the tiniest looks.
I am a father to him, his claws,

not a father any other way.
I take him in my humoured arms
and sleep half an August day.

ALL THE SONGS

It's just a Will Young song,
Like it's just a funeral
Or wedding, to paraphrase
McGimpsey, who always knows
How the popular can gong
Where the merely lofty
May be unheard, or miss
The space where hearts go
In human remains; to review
The play, it's September,
That dying month of sorrows
Mixed-up by Indian rays;
The days continue, seasons
Are just a simpleton's way

Of marking the race's start –
The short run that never ends,
Except in the grave, to paraphrase
The poet who wrote about
Classical themes, but transposed
Them to a contemporary day –
So, it's just Will Young, singing
And I don't sing along, except
Inside I sort of do, and it
Makes me think of you, across
London, working elsewhere,
And the mere distance touches
A gentle spot, not maybe a nerve,
But it makes the tune curve out

Past Lord's wickets and howzats
To the station Florence Nightingale
Met the worst war-injured at,
Where she demanded be built a permanent
Canopy from the trains to the hospital,
So young soldiers wouldn't get caught
In the rain of that nightmare era;
The song brings you nearer; her kindness
Reminds me of you even more, darling.
History sings like a choir, it combines
All the lyrics and exploding shells into one
Great crashing cacophonic melee;
Just like a tuning-up set of players
Ruining the music to get it finally right.

London, September 10, 2019

ON THE SUPREME COURT RULING AGAINST THE PROROGATION OF PARLIAMENT, TWO SONNETS

Rain is impartial, it falls
On the client, the accuser,
And the bewigged court,
Without favour, without fervour;
The rain functions like law,
It delivers its decisions
On days of death, days of birth;
It touches the heavens, the earth,
The in-between citizen;
Unlike snow, love or hatred
It never thaws; it flows
Where learned minds have led...
It arises, in distant tumult,
Above mortal struggles of those

Who would play gods to ants;
To go below Machiavel faces,
Reading past their blank pages,
As a void, to where morals plant
Forests that build up parliaments,
The wood that grows strong vaults.
Rain is not passionate,
It is sane, measured, sober...
You can drink the rain
Unlike wine, and not go wild;
Though sometimes, supreme,
It makes people run in streets
In what is only apparent chaos,
To partially plan, partially dream.

September 24, London, 2019

WHAT'S NEXT

Christ, when will this mini-apocalypse
vanish, like most elections,
into yellow history modules,
retro facades nuked once?
It's a production and a half, testing
nothing less than human patience;
populism always fails after it makes it,
a rock star in a Vegas hotel.
I am angry and sad together –
Sangry? Not sure, to be honest.

No one can be too gentle,
too sentimental, too emotive;
what's next will see to all that;
there's a push and pull
to the wheel that goes flat
like ginger ale, the Ferrari
and the Ford both kaput
one day, to be automotive,
engines are mechanical;
the flesh is vulnerable to fumes,

forces, burns, skidding faults;
it's the nature of nature
to be achingly beautiful, to be full
of dangerous attractors, rot,
all the denuded simulators loom
large just before their fall;
no climax without an anti-climax,
and I was once Max to 99;

fine, my mother left me outside
our apartment door, to make me

knock – she'd ask, who's there?
I'd say, an animal. Which one?
I'd reply, a cat. She'd unlock
it all in one swing, and let me back in;
oh it was splendid Eden in a block
of pretty barbaric flats; but in retrospect,
weird as hell. What was she on about?
Power is a cute game but sad, too.
I find the autumn a deadly stockpile
of heartbreak's cheap recall,

it all floods back with the rain,
discarded leaves, forlorn as safes
left in a Montreal boulevard's dingy drain.
Express whatever the fuzz you want to,
because where you're booked into,
there's not much music, debate, less buzz,
few if any dinner parties to speak about,
other than that one whose invitation
brings a definitive sense of abjection.
Obvious, but why try to complicate dread?

October 1, 2019

AUTUMN QUARTET

I

even the undead are alive
and so are the mannequins
on the high street in
the thriving lingerie shop
because everything is alive
and so is ai and nothing
is against the artificial
anymore because the divide
between what is inorganic
and organic is going or is gone
so the tissue is torn between
wire and grid, chip or ion;
electric digital bone flesh skin
all the vibrancies are fluent
and the fluidity is dynamising
the echelons of being across
futurities in enterprise or home;
we are a new superfluxity
as if reinventing aerodromes
to move like a triceratops
as we have modified pylons
to glow like deepsea octopi
with their own weird radiancy
so now death and life are mixed
fortunes and biology is a text
rewriting itself like a foxtrot tangle

2

To the patient on the lawn
vulnerably white in hospital attire
your darker face set off by eyewear
that movie star-like obscures

only your identity not your desire
we see you sat in the hi-tech
wheelchair in sun this autumn day

the violent green beneath the tyres;
I want to take a phone pic
for Instagram but refrain out of

humanity or fear you could be me –
a twinge of empathy rare these days
how alone you are out in the blunt air

near sliding doors and hand gel machines;
you're seen as cured or fated to succumb
I hope your future is to be better than

the common run – wish luck to you stranger
stuck like a thumb in the open door
of vision to be hurt by caught seeing
or unharmed by artful surgery.

3

These great sad days of autumn
everything feels New York or school,
is revivified and made important
by a renewed sense the world is
about to have an audience with you
around the corner, if you are wearing
the proper shirt or eyeglasses, own
a fine pencil and smart pencil-case.
Love or romance operate nearby,
the weather is involved, cooperates
in the apprehension of an affair
of state or heart; nations clash
but the magazines are crisp
and the new books are all the rage
like leaves are red to fall in this age
of instant change or notoriety;
it buzzed and is sharp and here –
a fresh this is itness that dares
your spirit to take risk and care
for any passing hound or fiend
along these moneyed avenues.

4

my lamb is gentle
my lamb is good
i come from a hospital
in st johns wood
they took a scan
as parliament warred;
the leaves are blood
and my soul a flood;
if you see a scar
it is also a tear;
sew up the wounding;
the summer was dear;
God is my leper
so i keep skin near.
it is all appearing
as i walk here
and beautiful food
plentiful if far.

PRINCE

When I first read FT Prince
kissing the wound in Christ's
side as if evil itself was beautiful
I swooned, a kid, since
such ideas in sounds
were a fresh new thrill,
war words far from real,
a sense of men bathing
after battle a mere Christianity
of flesh and metal, eros
unleashing its sinuous coils,
as knowing did in a brief garden
somewhere exciting poetry.
My desire to express and expose
thoughts of the body, chills
aching to reveal their serpentine
manoeuvrings, a tremulous way
of wanting to both be, conceal.

DEUX

1. Bishop Berkeley said

a candle flame feels
no heat; God provides

the burning core.
How can a thing itself

contain fire's roar
and be the conflagration?

We can. The truth
collides with collision

as a furnace divides
raging from raging light

in severe gradations
of leaping severity.

Nature's free for all
blights identity, encoding

each particle in the else
that boils to a magnitude.

The mind sustains its own
water course, to flood infernal

visions of a roiling orb;
one drop of water held

by next to lift a salmon
over jags, runs, pools

to achieve inevitability
in what's personal, oceanic.

2. Truth

When I got the book from Amazon
feverishly ripping open the box

I found it inside but in Polish
a beautiful language I can imagine

but not one I currently read.
I was about to return it

the little bit of tree and ink
but I thought of Brexit, Poland, truth –

sat down to the future task at hand
starting on page one, putting a finger

silently, on each foreign letter, as if my life
depended on getting this right

like some translator sitting to turn my English
into his tongue for me to only go bring

it back again across the unguarded border
of words, that flow like goods no one stops,

or if they do, not for long; containers of poems,
prose, going about their business as if nations

were open books and we had nothing to hide
but the fictions we like to relate, the purpose

of telling tales to be unsynchronised, late, odd,
making the stranger close, us never just ignorant.

SEVERAL

My heart is several broken, and I am several sad.
The sun's a clouded messenger, and I am clotted cream.
My night's a waking ambulance, light's a faded dream.
I've torn too many pieces, my needle is bare of thread.

I fear that I am living, I know that I am dead.
The moon's a distant negative, dust a constant cloth.
There is no airless fire, there are no moneyed moths.
I love, who never happened, I happened, to be mad.

St-Lambert, 1984

SONG

We danced about the kitchen,
We went to see the moon,
We loved after the morning,
Our love went on past noon,
We bathed and sent the water
Rocking overboard, beckoned
To each other, got off on the floor,
And this may be for all time,
And this may be for now,
Yet love is first an enzyme
Before it is a vow.

FROM THE GOSPELS

I have avoided my master for the year.
Like a good servant who understands
A gentleman's temper, he has not come
Near. I have set a house of disordered

Rooms around him, yet he is clear
Of household debris. I have broken
His plate in half, taken the handle off
His cup, and set a hole there instead,
But he is full and breakfasts in bed.

It does not matter that I sleep, hiding,
In the garage, or only tend the neighbour's
Lawn. He has already forgotten, saying
I have known him, in disservice, all along.

DAY AFTER ELECTION DAY POEM

there's no Heineken language
that hits all the spots –
it is sad great news –
one nation's landslide
another seat's crushing
defeat; who can speak
for unintelligible masses
except a monoglot despot
or popular turn of hate;
December is bitter
and bright – election day
darkens like paganism
into night. The wolves
that bay are starving brothers.
We must lie to one another
to make even marginal gains.

14 December, 2019, London

INSPIRED BY LYRICS BY COBAIN

Give me Lloyd Cole after-world
So I can be pseudo-literate eternally;
Or let me ascend to the relative heights
Of Hipsway, to preside over flimsy pop
For a dirty fortnight and a half; then
Again, I want Blow Monkeys Valhalla,
May I enter into the kingdom of Kid Creole?
Fork over Fun Boy Three eternal life
So I may croon uselessly in Maida Vale
To the Latvian waitress who serves tea
Cold in a nice white pot to me.

HOW ARE YOU DOING?

I myself expect Eminem
to use Kobe's tragic
sudden loss of velocity
as a cheap allegory,
because the artistic
is voracious, a blood sport;
the Wuhan viral story
is killing me a bit, they advise
a hermitic avoidance of news;
the hem of the world's dress
is unravelling a mad skein;
all my mythic schemes balls
of wool and twine, one way
into a maze wherein waits
a defiant beast;
the great die too soon,
as well as the small.
Fire consumes the flying
and the crouching. It's
the 75th year since
the camps were liberated
by Sgt. Rock and Company B.
Their New Jersey eyes opening
at the inhumane human horror;
millennials who bicker
over the slightest twitch
of a web, how could they forget
that once life depended on momentous
acts of risk, to save, hide or ignore
the historic Minotaur that Midas

hid in his personally-constructed abyss.
2020 feels like a blindspot,
where one gets hit on a smart carriageway.
I am trying to hold my little life
together. It doesn't matter in the schematic
does it, if one more toxic rep
from the damaged brigade walks
the digital plank. *The Lord of the Flies*
boys are nothing on the brigands
who patrol the metaphoric airwaves now.
Cruelty has been ramping up.
It's not worse than in 1945. It's alive.
It pulses and comes back, a receding
gum. The teeth that are bared fangs
were in a baby's mouth, beneath
the pacific skin. It's about to begin
again, the theatric colossus
in which we toss and turn, the bed
half-made by gods, God, men, genetics,
a splicing that does more harm
than good, and somehow expects
us to rise each morning to grin,
hooping dreams for our own team.

27 January, 2020

POEM

I apologise for the power
I do not have;
I regret the flowers
I did not give;
I am sorry for those hours
I wanted to misbehave;
I am the bearer
of an unowned slave;
yet the bonds of a rain shower
remind me I too shave;
as a man I shall cower
and bow, and rave;
as a person I am nowhere,
a victim of the ancient cave
where my father and mother
taught me to throw a stave;
for eons I killed for that tower
that demands it saves;
now I see the sacred bower
made me a lowly knave;
all the blood I gave and gave
for a cup of wine gone sour.

February, 2020

DAMN, NOW NICHOLAS PARSONS HAS DIED

For Shane Carr

I am tired of being reactive, aren't you?
I am tired of toiling at the long craft
In order to reflect my instant sadness
On a daily basis. My job is your life
Magnified by our shared pain
As channelled through the new news.
I am talking poetry here, OK?
Milton was a bad blind boomer,

With uncomfortable opinions, Brexity.
I hate having to hate everything
Ever done in the name of an evil empire;
Therefore, my favourite character
In the latest *Star Wars* was the Irish guy
Who was a traitor to the Emperor
But still bad, but he helped anyway;
I like divided royalties, I mean, loyalties.

I am living through this period of history
With you, can you feel my empathy?
I am your word friend, in images shared
Frequently. Poems are verbose selfies.
I am so sad that death and time occur,
It ruins beauty in an endless wave of refuse.
Literally, we are poison on the lips of love.
Shakespeare was a troubling sort of man.

We have problems I am not laughing at here.
This is not a game of noting down things
That have gone wrong with the total sum.

I suck my thumb in my ongoing oral stage.
I am exhausted, probably grievously, by our age,
Which makes too many bully demands.
I am trying to engineer a new style, a form
Of address and redress that is just transparent,

The opposite of opacity, or irony – hiding
Precisely nothing, being just authentic, like
This generation's ideal aims. No more clever
Claims to dazzling authorities or sly gods.
I sing the only current muses that remain
In this poorly, urgent, concerned frame:
Of complaint I sing, and the arms of persons
Dipping into the digital wine-dark empyrean.

BLUE AS THE NIGHT

calm as the night blue
just happens
a chance every dusk
trees swimming in blue
not any blue
a careful blue
pretending to be
morning and dark all
at once, sky holding
its breath, hiding
from the moon, coming
stars, a brilliance
serene as an ancient
vase posing flowers
invisibly in gowns of time.
I am so at peace
now is my calmest hour,
as if life was only kind
and fire only roared over
gathered kindling
in a Vancouver firebasket.

SONG

Every song
has Jesus in it
if you look and listen.

All books are the good
one. Put away your pain
daughter. Put off, son,

your slaughter.
Sing the solo parts
like a choir,

stood in line beside
you on the tilting deck
of the godforsaken Titanic.

Sing and laugh in the spume.
Never lack.
It's a waste to hold on

to enemies or plans
to plot to get them back
in the ultimate turn.

Hate never floats much.
Twist the knife out
of your conniving days.

You're on a burning limb;
it is breaking. Beside you
is the shackled glad king.

If that's okay for him then
you know what to do.
Accommodate, singer.

The battered treehouse
is your shattered inheritance
in the whirlwind. Be kind,

oh, plus, never hesitate
at the ludicrous gate
that tries to constrain your fate.

MANIFESTO

If you knew how to read
you'd know I was the real thing,

the king of passionate overflow,
fighting rhetoric with rhetoric,

melodramatic royalty bringing
emotional flooding to the ragamuffins,

prince among the soldiery,
each rousing speech a specific

momentous interjection, utterance
a defiance, a making of something

from breaking, a pick-me-up
for the gin-smashed peasants;

I am the boy gored in the central ring
by the bull you sent going,

critics of the dangerously human,
upsetting apple-cart-tipper;

I'm out of control except that's crap;
like tea, I get stewed with care;

I'm no more mechanically berserk
than the age we're broadcast in;

I am a very immediate mediation;
your toxic thief, cuffs glowing;

but the mayhem in my mayhem
is madness in the eye of the mania;

it's evocation, sirs, re-enactment –
disorder is one of the arts, a way

to convey the world's windstorms
on a page or staged display – it's

actoring, ladies, ungentle maybe
but crafted to open a gusting window

onto the rough hills where entire armies
fling their arms about the love they've lost.

My father, well, say no more, but
I do say more – no silence on brutality,

on inebriation's difficult un-mendings;
or the ones who meddled with my kidhood;

perversions and brain cancers demand
ululations – too much praise is given

to the stoic, the poised, the measured voice,
as if inculcating eloquent skeltering

was not also a formal choice – some rend
their dress as biblical expression of grief;

I mourn in metrical tottering, eccentrical
turns against whatever grain you've got –

I'm strong in a weakness of surprising
revelations of what's apparently careless,

yet random sound is often a bird's keenest
song, and all who care to listen

reach the same
lofty perch

in vertigo-singing
despite laws bent.

February 17, 2019

FOUR EIGHTS

Another confession, from another ex-confessor,
Seeking easy blessings, in an ultra-infectious world,
Knowing full well the leaders are cocks-driven,
What image for the tumbling of the Roman arch
Has not been offered as proof of poetic vision?
All or nothing, the choice for the God-crazed ones,
And these years feel especially spoken to by zeroic
Tongues, pierced by the calorific oralities of power;

I'm guttered, guttering, sputtering, a spitfire spitting
Blood, on fire, wings akimbo; I'd like to crawl back
Into limbo, a crushed foetal ouroboros, an amphora
Of myself, safe-salved in inner-scaped transfixiation.
I'd be a failed state if I was a genuine nation,
The dispossession is a displacement, I'm vague,
The mind has molehills, phobic without hermetic seals;
I fear competent death because I am unwilling to die well;

My smallish soul is hemmed in by its own needlework,
I've torn my heroic golden uniform to silly shreds;
I drift-sleep, demonic argonaut, as if hate was a bed;
I'm inept, slick-slipping off the deck into a churning
Dolphin-wrecked maelstrom; sailing to add hominem,
Me-directed ruination, my own eye is Charbydis, Scylla;
I'm the straits I'm in, the Antarctic of swinging poles.
I'd pray out to thee, but the emptiness is still appalling;

I wanted so much more, got less, that's the sin to address;
I spend too much down time reflecting upon what's real;
There's a fundamental architrave to fix, despite unruly
Desires ruling our plumblines and mortar; mortal, build
A bestering stadium to loft where pillars quake
At the westering core of an intractable spoiled field.
I am the dangering resource of my own festering yield;
Christ in your professional multiform join me on this job.

February 17, 2020, London

FR. OLIVER LEAVING

Father, I walk with you to Paddington,
In the rain, over the bridge, to the Heathrow
Express, after a day of talking about love,
Forgiveness, and how you married the Travellers
But then some Holy Joe called them scum.
You've been the unspoken saint, the kind one,
It's taken a toll. I know. I'm a sinner,
But I share a sense that love is required

At the end and the start of any life.
You made us man and wife. You've fed me
With Christ. Once, back from Rome,
At eighteen you returned to your family's farm,
And your sister's friend said, look how
He glows, how his skin's been burnt dark
Like a movie star. But as a boy, then man,
You turned from what could have been –

The joining of bodies in agonising pleasures.
The one loved, twenty-four, died holding your hand.
It wasn't a demand, what made you a priest –
A calling yes, but had the cancer not destroyed
That summer's fragile courtship, you might be a father
Of a different kind, now, a grandfather. Instead,
I'm a son of sons, daughters, not by blood or seed.
Need brings me to you, and insatiable instability,

A greed for balance, to be on the drip of chaos and good.
You'd include the excluded, love the unloved,
Shop in any shop, despite what they believed.
Your bravery's invisible to the secular eye.
You're the man who'd never hurt a malarial fly.
You'd rather die. I've never known a gentler person,
You embody, and it's absurd, what Jesus was,
The most-human, most-caring, most-unselfed,

Yet you're shy, and eat barely, down to fifty kilos,
All bone and on-call work mania, driven by absence
To fill the space with what you can do instead.
I love you as if you were Christ's light himself,
As you leave on the train, I think of our talk,
What it's like to be shamed, lost, cancelled, broken,
How time's sped, and know that some communion
Is humble, homespun, but raises the leftover bread.

February 20, 2020

LONELY DANCES

I think sometimes, if not often,
About the DJ who used to play
His records at the university dances.
Back in eighty-six, he was thin,
Wore jeans and a black turtleneck,
Specs I think, maybe that's window-

Dressing: he was the best,
But be careful, this was before,
If just, maybe it was eighty-four? –
Before the second summer of love,
Ecstasy – though XTC's pop was it,
And his selections were uniformly

Cool – I mean, judiciously chosen
To encompass his narrow passions.
It was mainly ska, 'Mirror in
The Bathroom' always – some slower
Reggae to chill the dark room –
Oh, the room – just a cafeteria

Nightened with no lights, the glass
Looking onto the ill-lit campus
(before campaigns started for safety) –
We'd dance, the young men in suits,
Skinny ties, some Docs, not many,
The young women in – can you

Believe I can't remember – I barely
Transfigure an imagining into dark

Dresses, some skinny jeans; beers,
In some hands; some weed, shrooms,
A taste in the mouth akin to pre-vomit,
And knowing the walking home

With a faint smell of snow around,
Alone, the sad complete thrill
Of dancing while the DJ nodded in his cans,
So pleased to introduce his small crowd
Of disparate students to his lean tastes.
I really danced for him, I loved him,

Never spoke to him, except to request
The Beat, which I knew was his favourite.
I was too shy to dance with anyone
From my classes, it was entirely solitary
This being eighteen, it felt far away
Even then, it is closer now, as darkness

Closes in again to my mind; I'd go
With him immediately, my forgotten
Pied piper of those remote Loyola
Scrums, the lost theology of those events,
Unless someone made someone pregnant,
And the birth lead on to prime ministers,

Junior ministers, banking, or mass murders.
For me, then and now are both confusing,
There's a time to be seeking for a friend
That doesn't find one, and for me
That was called all the time
I've been around.

NEW POEM WHILE LISTENING TO THE NEW MORRISSEY SINGLE

I know it is verboten to listen
to the rotten demi-Irish patriot, but
he's on Spotify, and has backing
vocals from a soul singer, so
I somehow give in, thus hear
him spracht-sing 'little Joe in the snow...',
but at the same time, I'm planning
the best way to self-isolate
in a *12 Monkeys* suit and
is any one else thinking Superspreader
was a band from Wales? No?
Well, I did. So there. Is great music
meant to be shunned, just because
the musician's a shit? Frank Sinatra
was. He once threw a hooker
from a window into a pool, not knowing
the pool was there (a joke reprised
in a Bond). Anyway, Covid-19
sounds like a paperback I'd avoid,
though I tend to read outbreak things;
play Pandemic. I shocked the monkey,
ratted on the rat; but I cannot outfox
the fox. I can't take anymore, darling
to paraphrase Gabriel. It's a comorbid
moniker. I would like to extend
my sympathies to all those in face-masks;
all those buried in lead caskets;
I am confusing infections and radiation.
Like you, I was born into a body, go

forth into an unsafe zone peopled
with monsters, the ultimate Dungeon
and Dragons set-up; but the master's gone
insane, and all the children are screens.
The news is not breaking, it's broken.
The bible has spoken. This is ending.

12 February, 2020

SHUTTING SHOP

The body shutting down,
The storm coming,
The cyclone in the blood,

On the news, warnings,
To nail up the boards,
Take what you can carry

Before it comes and takes
It all anyway; there's a finally
Gentle sense of returning

To where you're known most
In considering packing up,
Locking the doors with piano

Wire, using hockey tape
On windows any kiss would break,
So the shop's already a past, it's sad

But what else to do, in a small
Town when the radio calls out
That the end is on the fast road,

Just close the shop, go somewhere
Where there's only your defeated ones,
Who lie in some other consideration,

Who once had their locks to abandon;
The white is blinding now, it's cold calm,
You've got a huddling coat to walk with,

You've a barely mentioned name,
Bringing less than expected, it feels
Very decisive, clean, this barebones

Nothing is required, just get out,
Close those lights, get on your bike,
Wobble out from advancing disaster, say:

For everyone I'll forget when dust,
There are new ones I'll meet, I trust.
I'll open a store again some way I must.

18 February, 2020

TEARS FOR FEARS

It's not fashionable
to claim to love 'Raoul
and the Kings of Spain' –
but I need to make it plain:

this is the full bliss,
Tears for Fears unspooled;
how to name the kiss
that changes a fool

or contain how music
destroys, cool, as it maintains,
a missed word, pulls
it in again; all songs come

from heaven, all critics from hell;
that is why the fusion's unstable.
The kids of misrule could tell
you why pop remains

long after the nuclear station's
pooled out its pain, mangled
the plains, with lavish deforestation.
It's a thrill-kill mission, demolishing

all that's less than a game, it's
pure miss-and-hit, it's a dating kick,
the rush of saccharine, strychnine;
top of any list is always a green

smear of complaint, adoration, sick
licks, total output, the whole thing there –
madhouse, sure, but not ambiguous –
this song rollicks, it unrolls, it's

grindhouse, little Satan, jean stains,
boy racers without breaks, lasses
turning on the floor like spinning tops;
the hop begins with chaos, never

ceases to be the sea, beyond
the bounds of faith or family. All
that's fun, ludicrous, and insane
rings around posing vinyl like Jenny.

PRAYER IN TIME OF COVID-19

'didn't it rain…'

I have been a wasting space
Of do nothing but what I felt
Like, a raised lazy son of a dog,
A broken log, blazing with me,

Fully thrown from your tree,
God, in your in-particular
Hard to disagree with ways,
Hold me now as I await the days

Of a coming viral infection
That enthrals the community.
I have no pension, squandered
Recklessly, a drunk squirrel,

A wastrel, as I said above,
I have ill-deserved lovely love,
Been lonely, then satiated,
An unjust cause, a blown thing,

A barely sentient piece of dross,
A flawed string fraying at knots;
A blot on the paper of the good book;
A sour look, a groaning grain,

A busted flash in the rusted pan;
A backyard ambling wayward man.
I didn't give the kind gifts to my lady,
I didn't stay in the sun, went shady.

I stole our share of the gravy.
I went crazy for fun, unwarranted
Mania my way of biting too much fruit.
I could have done great works,

Fed the unhoused, built hovels
For the lowly, grown corn for the unborn;
Torn the porn from the pages,
Painted the walls with stripes of glory.

I am sorry. I have been ages numb
When feeling was required; squired
My sins to the party like a waiter
High on free coke. I've been a dirty joke

On the lips of a daughter; I have driven calves
To the slaughter after ploughing the lemmings
Off the cliffs with a tractor in the documentary.
I have deceived my maker, admired the faker,

Sat and ordered sexy wine with fools
And the criminally trepanned; I have planned
For lust, without caution; I drank the orphanage's
Milk. I tore bits from her silk.

I wore sunglasses at the funeral, and bit
The crown of thorns to taste the Lord's sweat.
I have placed every lousy easy bet,
Slept with seahorses when the seahouses

Were locked. I fingered doomsday clocks,
Confused times; I made up rhymes,
And diddled the devil for instant gratification.
I dined at high tables with smug atheists,

Mocking the Calvary ruts; I stoned sluts,
Claimed taxes for unkempt businesses.
I falsified witnesses; stole names from tombs;
Waged war on wombs; confused Telemachus

With Telecon. I am Jim Bacchus and Moriarty,
Luther and druthers, big brothers, small minds.
I pulled down the sun blinds; drove the cop car
Off the main roads, into the flood.

I drank pig's blood and ate pearls with twine.
I lacked the nous to undo the noose,
Set loose the demons, then drugged the choir.
I set the altars on fire with napalm.

I smeared my genitals with healing balm
For all the wrong reasons at holy week.
I was, always, a weak, self-focused dimwit
Who only pretended to give a shit.

I did justice for acclaim, charity for applause.
I observed merely the convenient laws.
I am built up from an anthology of flaws.
I await the coming storm of deaths with terror.

I could have built cathedrals in the clouds,
Inspired blind and deaf wandering crowds,
Made plays, statues, poems, better clauses;
Raised observant families, celebrated calm.

It's way past too late at this deserted stage.
The poverty of the hour is stark raving clear.
Oh, Christ in your total abject bizarre kindness,
Somehow bubble the world from the rushing-in

Parasite on the aerosol foam;
Make us near to your wounds;
Let your scarified kids
Saunter brazenly home.

16 March, 2020, London

AND COVID SHALL HAVE DOMINION

all that was
to be considered
an order of magnitude
no bigger than capital
all changes
was ever so
it came upon a holy night
at least in Christendom
knowing no borders
demanding borders
silent king of smallness
obligate parasite
no evil in universal
motion only chemical
transaction as design
velocity the arrow
everything grows or dies
it is natural to spread
a flowering tree
or locust blossoms
the valleys are silent
the citadels and perimeters
still, hoarded toiletries
the human collects
we are alone again
this is the new coming
Eden has returned
eat of the final tree
this fruit kills
but solitude injects time

to recollect
the ages built of anguish
and medicinal properties,
rose blush and tenderest
kissings, passion of the book;
what is not infected
is infecting; no immunity
in a world of connecting
tissue

THAT TIME REMEMBERED

Something about duty, about going into the sun
As if it was rare; something about not enough
Of basic things, too much information;
A recollection of locks, distance, and crowds
In parks as if they were safer. A sense the young
Were careless, indifferent, as they always are;
The old preparing for what they knew happens;
A time of waiting, as if the air raid sirens

Had just begun, but the shelters hadn't yet
Flung open. Something else, connected to being
Apart, a decision we made to come together,
A grander union, after division bells, local anger;
Seriousness at a level you could hear in a stadium,
But they were shut. The image of someone holding
A pint glass, laughing at the figures on the telly;
Stocking up on boxed sets, brown rice, macaroni;

Wondering if the straps of your mask were right;
That clutching in the chest like holding on
To your last belongings; a gust of fight or flight.
More dying than had to, but that's politics,
A retired nurse leaning over with exhausted fear,
Back for a final act of compromised immunity;
The blue ventilator wheezing, or was that her?
Funerals without mourners, that enclosing year.

22 March, 2020, London

ON THE VALUE OF READING DURING A GLOBAL PANDEMIC

Though it saves no life
passes time
that could be wasted
with *Money Heist*
or *Tiger King*
on Netflix; or fear

or breaking the law
with walking twice
the same day. To read
is to return
to somewhere never gone
or only in memory;

it is a home abroad,
a power without pain.
Libraries are banks
that never drain away
their fiscal strength;
a book is a mile

of miles at a single length.
You may start Sir Browne
and die before the *Urne*;
no holiday ends
too late; life is brevity,
reading infinite. We zoom

the stone of ourselves
upon the surface of time
like a meteor burning
as it skips the skin of space.
We hold a place
to return again. But even

entering the waves once
permits the wetting sea
to begin. Death is omnipresent,
gasping at medics
like a vicious shark; they lean
in to serve, are swallowed

themselves by dark.
Though lovers break orders
to couple danger in the park.
Open any volume, intake
the giving breath of a moment
whose endless living

is language's flowing monument.
No consolation consoles
enough to kill contagion;
philosophy knows without force;
still in the textual course
we stand and receive words

to surpass life or death
in omnipotence which plenitude
bestows on merely
temporary things that bare
swords or teeth at war
or love or both or all.

26 March, 2020, London

I SAW MY FIRST FLOWER TODAY

not only of this spring
but ever
as this time my eye

saw at once
what might never be
seen later if I might die

the next day
as the time is fast
coming of a blight

so the red rippling
flew out at me
like a wild thing

so enraged with living
it seemed no cage
could keep such a tiger in.

READING LAURA MULVEY'S LATE STYLE ESSAY ON *VERTIGO* IN THE LIGHT OF COVID-19

She says that film is death
in its each frame, moving
life into motion by light
so artifice plays on reality,
arousing automatons,
those herky-jerky objects
we desire to own, infuse

with fake breath, because
to dominate the unreal
is what only gods, artists,
do. In *Vertigo* Madeleine
is memory, crossed twice,
a favourite bridge, she's
ordinary spouse refused,

credit card declined, turned
as in *Pygmalion* into goddess;
she falls doubly, is a double
image and the pain is fetishes
are never again what they once
were in the possessing hand;
you play, let go, released

the toy breaks on the rocks
below. Freud, Adorno, the one
who died at the Swiss border
and loved unpacking books,
Benjamin, the master theorist
of machinations and creation;
the late style is, Deleuze or Said

both knew, an outcropping
of what's placed behind us,
the time before the mastery;
the backdrop replacing actual
smashing waves with fashion;
how we make up and dress
plain Mom to become Marilyn

Monroe. One blonde icon falls
into another one, Russian dolls
as German ghosts in American
films as desired by French eyes;
there's no meprise only error
and decline. In the silent streets
of London now no Ripper stalks,

no Hitchcock strangler taking
lives; the obsession is ours
with disease, invisible so pictured
in disguise as national trauma,
the dream of attacked glories
remembered as any sex sin is;
not since the war... rationing,

sacrifice, Nightingales... images
respliced to fit a new purpose,
until we almost find it beautiful,
this still distant strange alien
world we're woven back into –
reborn into the uncanny made
definition of sci-fi terror –

the 1950s when *Touch of Evil*
and all the saucer flicks appeared;
invasions, panic, fear, control –
only icy command, medical poise
will save us from our own urge
to lean far from our towers, girls
flung to fanciful destructions

by going out with someone twice
our age or more than our families;
wash hands, avoid touch, reality
kills. In seclusion, we're reborn
as robots that can survive on air,
eat only news. We're movies,
silent, stilled, with the projector

temporarily broken, as is society.

2 April, 2020, London

MISSION NIHIL

I shot the nihilist in the face
With the Glock when I met them
On the mutiny road; observed

The bleeding out. It was a starless
Evening, and nobody came out
To assist. It was a clean kill,

More or less, and, godless.
I went on to town on my stead,
Tethered Leopold to a white van,

Went into the laundromat
To swiftly silencer another man;
A good night for work; and clean

Shirts, to boot. I am not Groot.
I am a *kompromat* gone rogue.
Less talk, more subs in recycling bags.

Met the slim demonologist outside,
Ice-picked their human heart,
It spurted normal surprise.

Call the number, win the big prize.
Give me the name, I'll do the rest.
Save the last for best; visited

The lousy little publisher of porn
Fictions, all incest Kropotkin nonsense,
Yeats messed up with Crowley, a shit,

Crushed his head with a titanium bat;
My chimp says hi, Mister No Need For A Hat.
It's fun massacring the flat affect creeps

Who don't believe they have anything
To look forward to in the afterlife;
It's my financial irony to profit

By shunting them dead easy a bit early
To their indifferent pits of coiled snakes,
Or despoiled virgins, or vomit-encrusted

Urchins; skinny-shaking brides from Hanoi;
I'll do a general, a rich guy, some presidents,
But the deviant dolts who jerk to dead

Pics of the camps, or perv at lynchings, go
To the core of what's the joy of my job:
There's meaning in annihilating nothings.

SEARCH WEBCAM

Temporarily out of stock
Like we're out of commission
In this suddenly most-important
Universal level ultra-documented
Wankfest triple lockdown without pity

In a pretty shitty city of the dumbed-down
Have a badge and some garbage bag PPE sit-
Uation, all fooked-up, no-normal the new-control
Group, we've become epidemiologists, covidiotically
Holding forth, as never-surpassed isolation exposers,

Poseurs heightened to distinction-level *self-focusants*;
I mean, we've been fed the oxygen of living in important
Vassalage, enslaved-in-situ by our demanding spy handlers,
Who want us to check in constantly with new recipes, talks,
Zoomed-up unzipped ongoing temperature checks, moans –

Only the bereaved, the old, the sick, the dying, newly-recovered
Have a legitimate story to express, and the noble carers, but the rest
Are just careerist entryist lickspittle bastards, profiteering busybuckets;
And because of them I can't Amazon a rescue package of 1080p HD 360
Mic-included plug and play *ConstantLife* silver two-way conferencing night

Vision tech; the levee's going to break, without any means to capture it all;
The fall of mankind and I'm stuck here alone, with only a frickin smartphone.
My epic requires a Chicago-style steak and bluesman Led Zeppelin riff as it ends;
My plan was to cast like the sequestered porn stars health-safety-distancing in LA
A Chinese-drip-feed of autofocus streaming natural me, Wordsworth to his friends.

April 16, 2020 London

CICERO UNLOCKED

After D.T. with love

Cicero knows a soul is there or isn't there
And neither bandage unbreaks the fear;
My cat's coalfired sleeping in a fiery pool
Put out in purrs sleep derails, his fur
The kingdom of panthers all breeders confer
Ribbons on; in heaven the dead move too –
In puzzled sleep, at their side some owner
Scribbling also of the worried times: half
The world is half apart from half the world's
Other part – the solid heart has come to know
The dialogue of self, and loss, and selfless loss;
As Plato told, and Aristotle tossed aside, in scorn.
We're divisions of an army made up of us
Alone; the hill-town's been cut off from its face,
To save the sloping nose to keep the mills alight.
Economies of scale collapse

      like climbing bibles
Tipping off a feeding beltway to appal the stars.
It is dust bowling as dollars fly like mice
Out of the cat hospitals to die church poor
In single pairs of lost mittens, disallowed to mourn
Until morning's dark and the mountains flat as ice.
We split hairs like Moses, slit the camel to accommodate
The eye – our needles are threaded by Threadneedle,
So more of less, and less of more, can safely die –
As if death was money, words blunt tools, and life a lathe.
The brave are folding up their safety pins to save
Mere dying ones who turn on a causing cough;

Bosses dine on podium broadcasts like birds join bread
On lakes; numerical troughs are gouged in hills that rise,
Decrease, decease – slumping's made us all apocryphal
As Pythagoras' tall tales figured by figmented beads –
The world's a model standing on an angel's tip-toes.
We're in the counting throes of death too numerous to have
Numbering; we stop at ones and zeroes to defy binary
Needs or broad naming of particular, infinite complexities;
The singular taxes the treasury, the task force grapples
Like a misfit crampon, loose as lynchpins in bald flight.
Cry, Zion, for the solitary mister and miss in a middle,
Muddled in separation on a kinging quiet street, missing fools.
Half the world's a blasted safecracker bent to his thunder
At a blowing carnival when the banking jig is pinwheeled.
Clap for carers who care less for their own primal skins
Than ours, be insane on Thursdays out of doors, mayhemming
Lest the gowned fabric of our society frays, baying
At an endless moon of boring concentrated fear,
Frowns into nothing from everything despaired.
O, Jupiter, alter our banal corpuscles, test us shaking,
A tree torn from leaf

      or wind to be clarified;
We're poised like ancient gigolos to do little,
Or suddenly spring loaded into action's cage –
Diving from a deadly platform to a waiting room;
From puddle to emergency, to struggling depths;
As Cicero promised you, Death that courses
Has no cursing channels past the sensual body;
Pain is livid or not much to discern – the dead
Oblivious to oblivion, in the final sea see nothing,
Flowing out of health up to heaven's numbing,
Lethe's leading waters to the drowsy gentleness

Of being born before Genesis struck nails –
As if storks raced backwards to beat a clocking sun,
Solar scatter – all God's apple seeds sewn across
London's grown eyelids of
      a blind starveling Raven-thief.

April 18, 2020, London

DELAY, CONTAIN – 1% OF 80% WILL DIE...

It takes China
To close a city
Doctors are martyrs
In infected Iran
Deny is England's way
Lockdown Italy
The Pope on TV
Saved by Screens
It's all hermetic

The mafia sells passes
Like in *Casablanca*
You can cross the alps
To superspread
Among the cuckoo clocks
Of Lake Geneva,
Hiding radiating Nazi gold;
Only the underlying old die
Or as many as in WW2.

The smart epidemiology
Is up for debate on Fox.
Hand gel sold out
Like a crazed date
In Kubrick's Vegas.
One expert says he fears
This one more than Ebola;
Other rock and rollas
Kiss and hug to defy
The numbers that don't lie.

It came from cave-bats
Into our general population –
Obligate parasite
Nice and sleazy does it...
The Ruskies blame the USA,
Going viral with fakery;
Once lies sunk ships,
Now they build campaigns;

It's biblical, it's end times.
It's romantic sublime; but
The lab like in Alistair
MacLean's *Satan Bug*,
Was 500 metres from Wuhan's
Live animal market –
Don't kill the whistle-blower
Holding the oxygen mask.
My ventilator's perforated;

There's even live porn
Featuring sealed suits
Last seen in *ET*, or *Contagion*;
It's a fetishistic hit parade.
Contain, delay, mitigate,
Research – experts declaim.
Safe behind their telly cameras;
Tom Hanks has come down
With the killer down-under;

If he goes, we'll name it after him.
One percent will die of Hank's Disease;
Collapse of airlines;
We're doing fine, luv;
Keep the matches packed;
Shove them into the pubs, mate.
I recall toxic Spacey
Cutting his Ebola suit
And dying in the tragic lab

In *Outbreak* – Dustin
Hoffman appearing tiny
As a commander.
I recall blood drying like sand
In *The Andromeda Strain*,
Only alkies and babies surviving
In the desert ghost town;
I grew up fearing those white
HazMat Bio Suits more than Nazis;

Keys was evil, wasn't he?
In OJ's greatest scene onscreen –
Why are all the disgraced actors
In epidemic B-movies?
The *Cassandra Crossing* combined
The two themes of this text –
The Holocaust and the World Health
Organization – machine guns
On trains, soldiers in those white

Protected uniforms of medical
Distrust – *X-files* sex dreams –
It's come to pass, the horror
Schemes, predicted by Frank Herbert,
The X-Virus, the hottest one,
The global zone, the final result
Of excessive experimentation
On alien DNA; these are Scully's
Monstrous children, wreaking havoc.

March 12, 2020

HOT ZONE CONFESSIONS

'Thomas and Lowell made themselves the metaphor of their poems'

1.
I am myself the quarantine.
The garden spreads children
In summer clothes like sores

On a lip. The world quivers,
All arrows locked and loaded
To overflow. I don't quite explode.

2.
Writing has never been bomb squad
To the great squatting missiles below
Our skins; you don't avoid

Volcanic eruption with lava postcards.
Words hurl microbial aerosol
Across the lawn to sicken, invade.

3.
I'm only paper, metaphor, inky myth.
What's made isn't mine or shrapnel to own,
Contains pandemics in its sly mists.

Controlled explosions like punking steam?
All dreams are engines to the minefield
Mind we try to civilly distance from, or collide in.

4.

We've died in rhetorical verse too often to see
The trees burst from it like shells out of
Burial mounds; all's fecundity, even dross,

Drivel, moss, or fungal rot. All personal works
Surround me, yet extend, like vines on branches
Furl in forests to the furthermost interior animals.

5.

Go out, stay in, be free to cower or to hide; release.
Impersonated by creation make a ruptured fortress
Of thy heart. Cauterise the world-wound's founding

Art. Sun extends its allegorical medicine to kill
Viral demons on our burnt lawns. Families intersect,
Breaking stricter laws like magicians will taboos.

6.

No decision today will lift the tension in the busy groves;
Cool hands sterilised, we've handed authority over to science
To judge on stony grounds. The hottest zone is inside ourselves,

With stocked salt, rice, ordinance unexplored on canny shelves.
The poem is the panther in the shade waiting for the kill.
She tenses before acting, like all powers, in fateful pause.

April 25, London, 2020

IN MEMORIAM, THE POET CIARAN CARSON

It's not for me to say
Anything to you
About the city
Or the music
Poetry made ring true.
Your tin whistle
Or your wife,
The wild nights

And ashen days
Of long gone tours
(to paraphrase Banville),
Are yours, all yours.
And not, now.
An obituary
Is a skinny stick
On which to lift

A life sky-high, a lie
In words, comparably,
Yet something drab,
If locally handsome,
Can come across
When a poet's died
In what is said
Of the unemotive dead.

The grim, grand trudge
Of Irish history, half-done,

Incomparably incomplete,
Though sung with whiskey neat,
Was in your head and street;
You took what you could find,
And then some, adding
From the local store,

To bridge a gulf,
Bind a limb, and recreate;
I can see you, almost,
And that almost is the cost
Of a vision getting lost
Amidst rubble time uncrates,
Like shattered statuary
Rescued from a civil fall

Only to be stumbled on
Among the craters of a bomb;
Well, I can see someone,
If not you, then them,
Picking his way through books,
In a November day dark so soon;
Seeing something at the window,
A figure outside the glass,

A shadow of himself,
Or just another Carson
Going past. Either way,
It's critical to say, fair enough,
You wrote good poems
Greater than the usual sum,
That thrown together, begin
To look grown by a green thumb.

ACKNOWLEDGEMENTS

Adrian Borland's song 'Winning' has inspired me in finishing this project – I thank his brilliant spirit.

WHAT OTHER CRITICS AND POETS HAVE SAID ABOUT TODD SWIFT'S EARLIER PUBLICATIONS

'[...] a dapper sense of style' – **Emily Berry**

'[...] a relentless drive to render dramatic discord with brilliant polish' – **Jason Camlot**

'[...] almost Jacobean richness of the diction, the surprising and graceful turns of the syntax' – **Bill Manhire**

'[...] exquisite timing and formal innovation' – **Luke Kennard**

'[...] uncommon panache and intelligence' – **Srikanth Reddy**

'A voice for our time' – **Derek Mahon**

'His voice is powerfully his own, but poetry lovers will find the grace notes of plainsong TS Eliot, but also the verbal dexterity of Robert Bringhurst' – **George Elliott Clarke**

'Savage and gentlemanly' – **Regie Cabico**

'Sincerity and comedy attuned to a subtle ear' – **Daljit Nagra**

'Such sexy bravado' – **Diana Fitzgerald Bryden**

'Swift has a beautiful sense of the rhythm of the English language' – **Pericles Lewis**

'Swift is a prodigiously talented and singular poet' – **Don Share**

'Swift's poetry is so evidently intellectual, witty, urbane and ludic that you think you know where you are, and then comes the night – some image of such chronic unease, you're unsettled entirely' – **Bridget Hourican**

'Swift's work is as playful as serious work gets to be' – **David Lehman**

'The intimate is always threatened: reality is challenged by its myths' – **George Szirtes**

'Todd Swift is a poet besotted with language and stubbornly working out a high style of his own' – **Al Alvarez**

'Todd Swift is a revelation' – **Terrance Hayes**

'Todd Swift is the real thing' – **Ilya Kaminsky**

SELECTED PREVIOUS POETRY
PUBLICATIONS 1988-2019

(note, not including academic or prose writing or critical editions)

Full Collections
Budavox: Poems 1990-1999 (1999)
Café Alibi (2002)
Rue du Regard (2004)
Winter Tennis (2007)
Seaway: New & Selected Poems (2008)
Mainstream Love Hotel (2009)
England Is Mine (2011)
When All My Disappointments Came at Once (2012)
The Ministry of Emergency Situations: Selected Poems (2014)

Selected Pamphlets and Special Editions
The End of the Century (1990)
The Cone of Silence (1991)
American Standard (1996)
Elegy for Anthony Perkins (2001)
The Oil & Gas University (2004)
Natural Curve (2006)
Unfinished Study of a French Girl (2014)
Madness & Love in Maida Vale (2016)
Dream-beauty-psycho (2017)
We Are All Weak & Crazy When We Would Repent (2018)
But Strong and Feisty When We Would Sin (2018)
There's an Excess at the Heart of Being That's Wild (2019)

Selected Anthologies, as editor or co-editor

Map-Makers' Colours: New Poets of Northern Ireland (1988)
Poetry Nation (1998)
Short Fuse: The Global anthology of New Fusion Poetry (2002)
Poets Against the War (2003)
In the Criminal's Cabinet (2004)
Future Welcome (2005)
Modern Canadian Poets (2010)
Lung Jazz: Young British Poets for Oxfam (2012)
The Poet's Quest for God (2016)

BIO NOTE

(Stanley) Todd Swift, PhD, is a poet, screenwriter, anthologist, literary critic and publisher. He was born on Good Friday, 1966, in Montreal, Quebec, Canada, and has lived since then in Berlin, Budapest, Paris and now London. He began writing poems seriously in 1980, inspired by the poems his mother read him regularly, and was soon published in magazines. He was a verbal prodigy, debating against university students when he was 14. He was soon the high school debating and public speaking champion of Quebec. In 2017-2018 he was for a year writer in residence, Visiting Scholar, at Pembroke College, Cambridge; and was third placed in the election for the Oxford Professor of Poetry, 2019. As a TV writer he was the series editor for *Sailor Moon*, and wrote episodes for shows from HBO, CBC, Hanna-Barbera and Fox. He has been a member of several writer's guilds and unions, such as The League of Canadian Poets, and the WGC. He was for many years the Oxfam GB poet in residence. He is married, and has many nephews and nieces, and a godson, Alex. He enjoys swimming, cross-x skiing, going to movies, drinking coffee, and playing with cats. He became British and Catholic in the last decade.